BLACK HOLES AND OTHER SECRETS OF THE UNIVERSE

BY CHRISTOPHER LAMPTON

Franklin Watts

New York/London
Toronto/Sydney/1980

An !mpact Book

Photographs courtesy of NASA: pp. 7 and 62; Hale Observatories: pp. 10, 21, and 30; American Museum of Natural History: p. 20; Lick Observatory: pp. 22, 47, 58, 59, 61, and 75; Kitt Peak National Observatory: p. 28; United Press International: p. 40; Yerkes Observatory: p. 41; New York Public Library Picture Collection: p. 52; and the National Radio Astronomy Observatory: p. 55.

The photograph on page 75 is of the Large Magellanic Cloud.

Library of Congress Cataloging in Publication Data

Lampton, Christopher
Black holes and other secrets of the universe.

(An Impact book)
Bibliography: p.
Includes index.

SUMMARY: Discusses black holes, what they are, why they exist, and the possible consequences they pose for our universe.
1. Black holes (Astronomy)—Juvenile literature. [1. Black holes (Astronomy) 2. Astronomy] I. Title.
QB843.B55L35 523 79-23306
ISBN 0-531-02284-6

Printed in the United States of America
5 4 3 2 1

CONTENTS

BLACK HOLES AND OTHER SECRETS OF THE UNIVERSE

PROLOGUE

There are places in the universe to which anyone can go, but from which no one can return. Places where time stands still, light travels in circles, and matter may become so heavy that it cannot remain in normal space.

There are objects in the universe that cannot be seen, but that can swallow stars, that even now might be eating our own galaxy from the inside out. There are objects that can tear spaceships and planets to shreds or cause explosions more powerful than a million atomic bombs.

These places, these objects, are called *black holes.* They are the burnt-out, superdense bodies of stars many times the size of our sun. They are surrounded by gravitational fields so strong that even light cannot escape. Inside these holes the natural laws of our universe may change, even break down completely. Passageways may open to other universes, other times. And, if scientists are correct, there may be millions, even billions, of them in our galaxy alone.

In a universe of logic and reason, the idea of black holes sounds crazy. But scientists argue that if such things do *not* exist, our entire concept of the universe may be wrong. According to theories worked out over many years, black holes not only *can* happen, but *do*. And they are happening right now.

Sound frightening? If it does, think about this: Some astronomers think that the nearest black hole may be no farther away than the star nearest to our sun, maybe closer. This is farther away than anyone will travel in the near future. Even if we could build a spaceship that would go that far, it would take hundreds of years to get there, much longer than the lifetime of any crew member.

But things may change. There could be spaceships in our future that will travel to the stars in weeks or even days. When this happens, black holes may pose a genuine hazard to interstellar navigation. In the far future, when space is filled with starships carrying passengers across the galaxy, encounters between human beings and black holes may be fairly common.

What will such an encounter be like? No one knows, not really. But we can guess.

You can guess, too, but first you'll need to know what black holes are like and why they exist.

CHAPTER ONE

What is a black hole?

It is a star that has grown old and run out of fuel. With no more fuel to burn, it collapses under its own weight. If it is a very large star, and therefore very heavy, it collapses with a great deal of force. It cannot stop collapsing. It grows very small and dense, so small in fact that it literally disappears from the universe.

But that is a simplified explanation, and not entirely true. To understand black holes more completely, you have to understand a few things about stars. And to understand stars, you have to know about atoms.

All matter in the universe is made up of atoms. Atoms are extremely tiny; they cannot even be seen, though they can be photographed using very special equipment.

But atoms are not the smallest things in the universe. There are, for instance, the subatomic particles which make up the atom. The most important of these, to our understanding of black holes, are neutrons, protons, and electrons. You do not need to know what these particles are like. Just remember that they are the building blocks from which atoms are made.

There are many different kinds of atoms. What makes one atom different from another is the number of protons, neutrons, and electrons it contains. Any type of matter that is made up of only *one* kind of atom is called an *element*.

Besides being made up of atoms, all matter possesses *gravitational attraction* (or simply, *gravity*). This means that all objects produce a force that causes other objects to move toward them. The strength of this force varies according to the size of an object and the number and size of the atoms the object is made of. Small objects—books or cars or even people—have so little of this attraction that you probably don't even notice it. But for large objects, such as planets and stars, this attraction is very strong. That's why when you leap up into the air you always fall back to the ground. The planet Earth, which you are standing on, is very large and therefore has a very strong gravitational attraction that draws you back to the ground whenever you try to leap away from it.

The amount of gravitational attraction an object has depends on its *mass*. The greater the mass of an object, the greater its gravitational attraction.

The mass of an object, in turn, is determined by the object's size and density. The denser an object is—that is, the more closely packed together its atoms are—the more massive the object will be, assuming that its size remains the same. By the same token, the larger an object is, the more massive it will be, assuming that its density remains the same. An object that is both very large and very dense, such as a mountain, will be very massive. An object that is not very large and not very dense, such as a wad of cotton, will not be very massive.

Mass is equivalent to weight, but only on the surface of Earth. An object that weighs 10 pounds (4.5 kg) on Earth's surface also has a mass of 10 pounds. However, if the object were to be taken into outer space, it would weigh nothing at all because it would be outside of Earth's gravitational field. *But it would still have 10 pounds of mass.* Mass is what gives an object weight, but it is not the same thing as weight. Unlike weight, it does not depend on the effects of gravity. An object's mass remains constant whether the object is on a planet's surface or out in space.

It is because of mass and gravity, and the effect of gravity on atoms, that we have stars.

If you go outside on a clear night and look up at the sky, you will see stars. The sky is filled with them, tiny pinpoints of light.

If you look at the sky during the daytime, you will not be able to see those stars. But you will see the sun. The sun is also a star. It seems brighter than the stars you see at night because it is so much closer to us than they are. It is so bright in the daytime, in fact, that its light drowns out the light from the other stars. That is why we can see other stars only at night.

Stars are very hot, so hot that we can feel the heat from our own sun across 93,000,000 miles (149,665,000 km) of space. What causes stars to produce such heat?

It is only in this century that scientists have begun to

understand what makes our sun—and other stars—burn. Most now believe that our sun formed from a large cloud of gas.

Five Billion years ago this cloud floated in space where our sun is now. It was made up almost entirely of the element *hydrogen*. Hydrogen atoms are made up of one electron and one proton. Like all other matter in the universe, these atoms have gravitational attraction, and therefore the atoms in the cloud began to attract one another.

As the atoms drew closer to one another, the cloud became more dense. As the cloud grew denser, it became smaller. The more tightly packed atoms began colliding with one another, creating heat through friction. As the cloud continued to grow smaller, more and more collisions occurred between atoms. The increased friction caused the gas cloud to grow extremely hot. When a certain temperature was reached, *hydrogen fusion* began.

Fusion is the same process that causes hydrogen bombs (sometimes called fusion bombs) to explode. Two hydrogen atoms heated to very high temperatures can fuse, or unite, to form a single *helium* atom. In the process there is a burst of energy, which shoots off into space as light and heat.

The energy given off by the two hydrogen atoms fusing into one helium atom is fairly small. The amount of energy given off by a large cloudful of hydrogen atoms fusing into helium atoms is tremendous.

Fusion caused the cloud of gas that was to become our sun to explode outward with the force of a giant hydrogen bomb. At the same time, the cloud was collapsing inward under its own gravitational weight.

The explosion prevented the cloud from collapsing al-

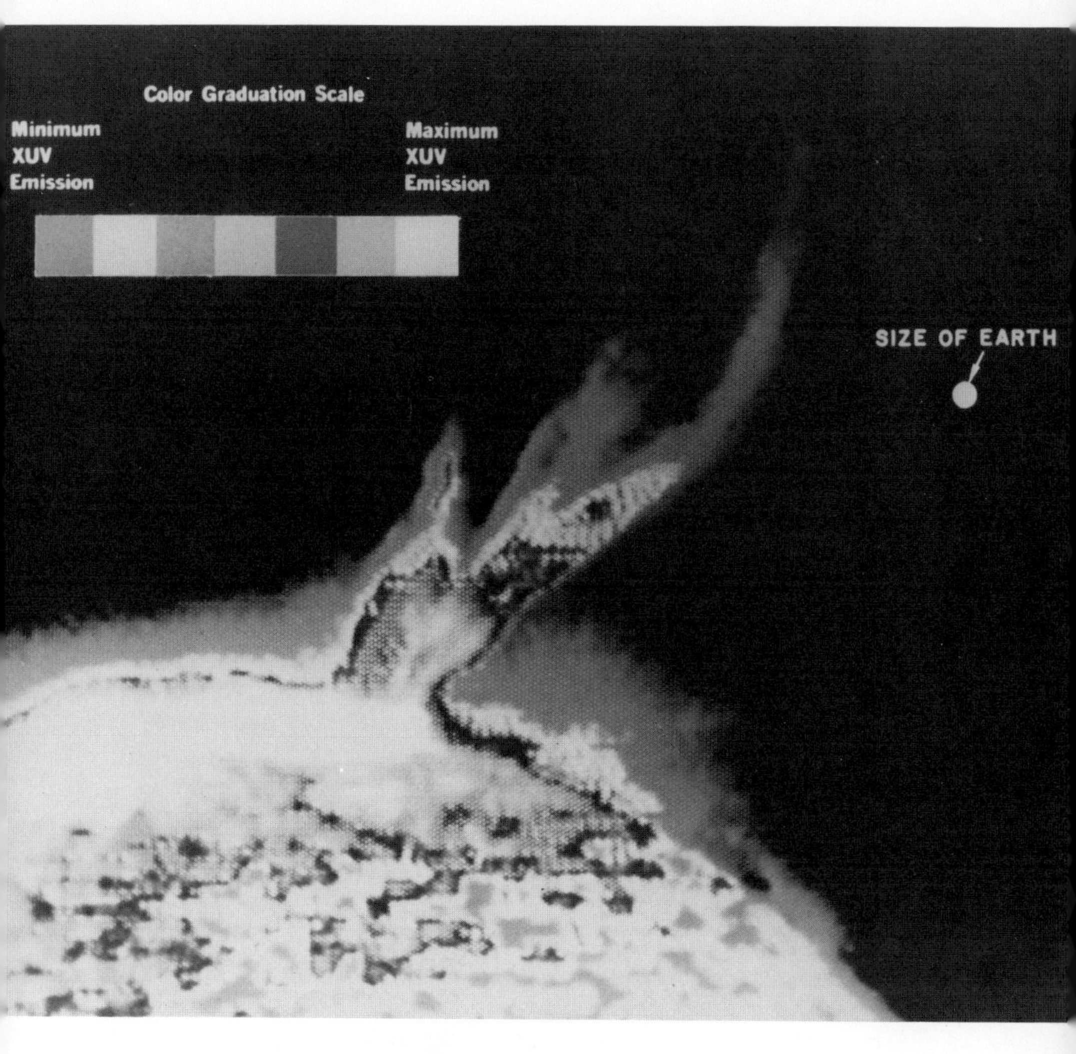

An explosion on the sun's surface, photographed from Skylab 3 *in 1973. Explosions such as this produce vast quantities of energy from fusion. The clouds of helium gas visible here blasted outward some 550,000 miles (880,000 km) into space.*

together. The gravitational attraction between the atoms prevented the cloud from exploding altogether.

At this point the cloud of hydrogen had become a *star*, our sun. And the process just described is exactly what is still happening right now inside the sun. At its core, hydrogen is still fusing into helium. This releases energy that works its way to the surface in the form of light and heat. The light and heat *radiate* (move outward in all directions) from the surface. Great quantities of this light and heat fall on the surface of Earth. Life as we know it would not be possible on our planet without this radiation from the sun.

There is enough hydrogen inside most stars to keep them burning for many millions of years. When the hydrogen runs out, however, they begin to collapse again. With no explosion at the core to balance the force of gravity, gravity takes over. This will happen to our sun in another 5,000,000,000 years or so. (The sun has already been burning for about that long, which means that its life is nearly half over.) Hotter, more massive stars burn their hydrogen fuel more quickly, perhaps in a few million years. Less massive stars than our sun may exist for as long as 200,000,000,000 years because they burn their fuel more slowly.

When a star goes into its second collapse (when it has become old), the friction from the tightly packed atoms inside it creates such intense heat that the helium atoms left over from the hydrogen fusion will begin to fuse into even larger atoms. The tremendous heat necessary to support this process will cause the star to swell up to many times its original size. A swollen star like this is called a *red giant*.

Because its core is so hot, the red giant will burn its helium fuel very quickly. After perhaps another 1,000,000,000 (or even fewer) years, it will begin to collapse again, producing even more heat. The atoms at the core of the star will continue to fuse into larger and larger atoms until no more fusion is possible. Now nothing can stop the star from collapsing completely, or *almost* nothing. It will collapse until it is so small that all of its atoms are crushed up against one another—and then stop.

Ordinarily, the atoms in a star (or in almost anything else) are very far apart from each other, relative to their own size. In fact, matter of almost any type is made up of mostly empty space. But after the star has collapsed, its atoms are so close together that there is almost no empty space between them. The matter of the collapsed star is very dense. It is so dense that a matchbox full of it would weigh 10 tons (9 m.t.). Because the star is now extremely dense, and its mass is packed into such a relatively small space, the gravity at its surface is extremely intense.

The collapsed star is still very hot, even though its nuclear furnace is no longer burning. Because it is still hot, it still radiates a large amount of light and heat. Astronomers call such a collapsed star a *white dwarf star*. After billions of years it will cool off and stop radiating. Then it will be a *black dwarf star*.

The collapse of the star is sometimes preceded by an explosion called a *supernova*. Often an old, very massive star will produce extremely intense temperatures in its core. These temperatures will be too intense for the star itself to withstand and it will explode. When this happens, great clouds of matter and energy are shot out into space while the inner part of the star continues to collapse. The amount

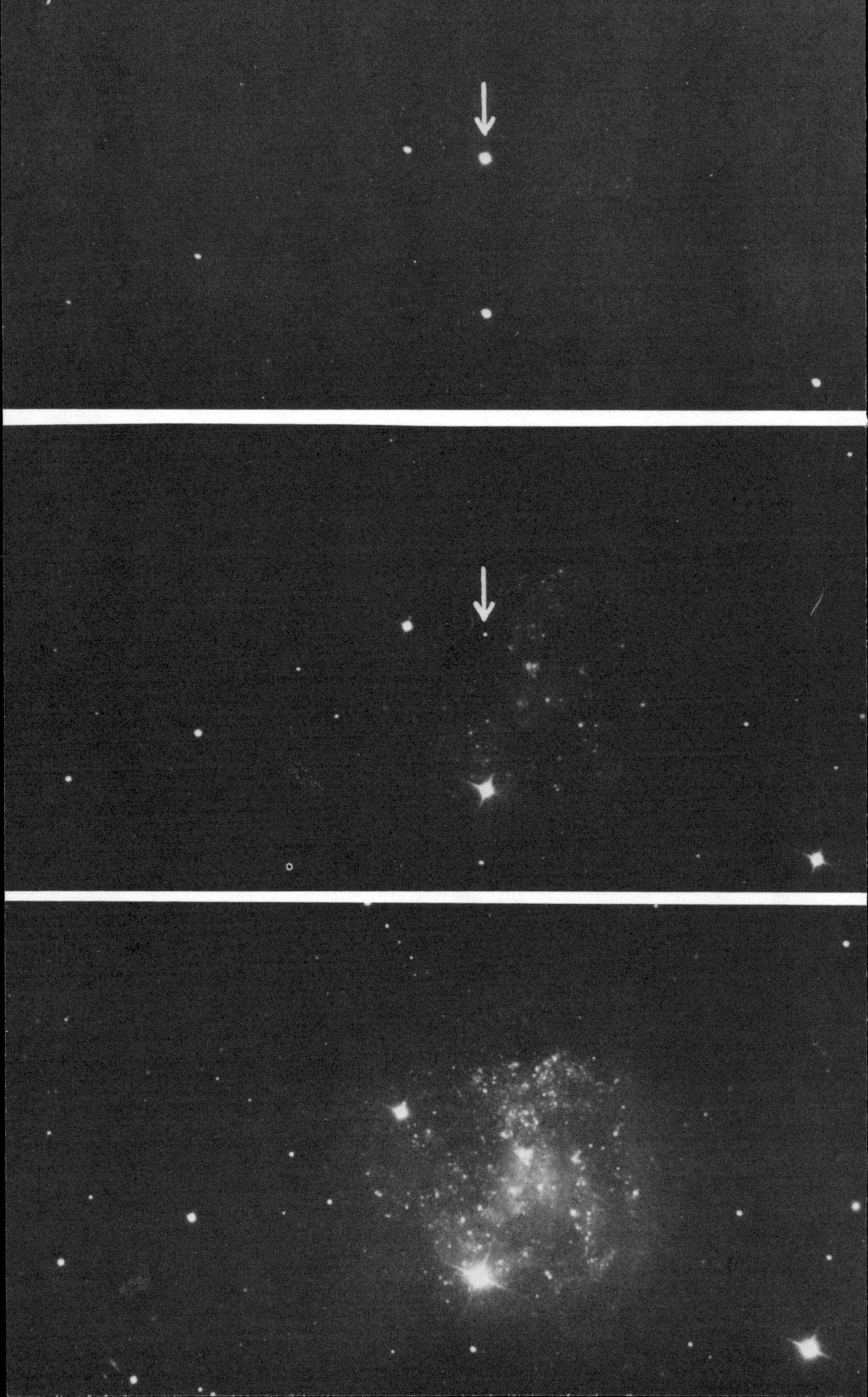

of energy released by an exploding star is many times the amount it normally emits.

You might wonder why a collapsing star reaches a certain size and then does not collapse any further. The reason is that the collapse is stopped by *electromagnetic force.* This is the force that holds the outer part of an atom together and keeps the electrons in their proper places. It is a very strong force, and if the collapsing star is of less than a certain size, the electromagnetic force will be stronger than the gravity that pulls the star inward.

But what if the star is very massive to begin with? Could the gravity causing the star to collapse become stronger than the electromagnetic force preventing it from collapsing?

Yes.

In fact, a massive star will continue collapsing, and continue growing smaller, even after it has reached the white dwarf stage. The gravity generated by the massive star will be so strong that it will overcome the electromagnetic force. This time the atoms of the star will collapse. The protons and neutrons and electrons will jam tightly against one another. The electrons and protons, because they have opposite electrical charges, will cancel one another out and become neutrons. (Neutrons have *no* electrical charge.) By the time the star stops collapsing, it will be made of nothing but neutrons. For that reason, such a star is called a *neutron star.*

A supernova photographed over a five-year period.

Since the force of gravity in the massive collapsing star is stronger than the electromagnetic force, what makes the star stop collapsing this time? The collapse is stopped by the *nuclear force*, the force that holds the inner part of an atom in place. It is what keeps the neutrons (and also protons) where they belong. It is even more powerful than the electromagnetic force.

Neutron stars are often no more than a few miles (1 mile equals 1.6 km) across. The matter of a neutron star weighs thousands of times as much as the matter of a white dwarf star. Its gravity is so intense that anyone who came into the vicinity of such a star would be torn apart by *gravitational tides*.

What are gravitational tides?

All objects in the universe have gravitational attraction, but that attraction grows weaker with distance. The closer you are to an object, the greater the effect its gravity has on you.

When you stand on the surface of Earth, your feet are more affected by the pull of gravity than your head is, because your feet are closer to Earth. The difference is so small, though, that you probably do not notice it.

When the gravitational attraction is as great as it is in the vicinity of a neutron star, the difference becomes more obvious. In fact, if you were falling feet first toward a neutron star, you would be torn into two pieces (at least!), because the gravitational pull on your feet would be so much greater than the pull on your head.

The same thing would happen to a spaceship or any object approaching the neutron star. Because this effect is similar to the one that causes ocean tides on Earth, we call it a gravitational tide. (Ocean tides are caused by the effect the moon's gravity has on the shape of Earth. This effect is small, of course, compared to the tides encountered near a neutron star.)

Suppose that our collapsing star is even more massive than the kind of star we have just been talking about. Suppose it is an extremely massive star, many times the mass of our sun. Would the force of gravity be stronger even than the nuclear force?

Again, the answer is yes.

There is no force in the universe stronger than the nuclear force *except* the gravitation from an extremely massive star. Therefore, such a star would not stop collapsing at the neutron star stage. In fact, it would not stop collapsing at all. It would continue to grow smaller and smaller and smaller—forever.

Soon, its gravity would become so strong that even light could not escape from its surface. From the viewpoint of a nearby observer, the star would vanish suddenly from sight.

It would become a black hole.

CHAPTER TWO

Suppose you were the captain of a starship, three or four hundred years from now. If you wandered into the vicinity of a black hole, what would you see?

Since light cannot escape from a black hole, the hole is in some ways invisible. But that doesn't mean you wouldn't see anything unusual.

For one thing, you would be unable to see the stars *behind* the hole, though you would not notice this unless the black hole were very large. The light from stars visible near the hole would be bent by the hole's gravity. They would appear distorted and out of place. It would look as though someone had taken a giant spoon and stirred the stars into a confused puddle.

If there were any matter in the vicinity of the hole, it would be immediately sucked into it. Like the collapsing hydrogen in a forming star, the matter would be heated to a white glow. From your viewpoint on board the starship, it would appear as if there were a bright halo of light around the hole. This halo is called an *accretion disc*.

The hole may be part of a *double star system* (also called a *binary star system*). A double star system consists of two stars orbiting one another. (Some star systems contain even more than two stars.) One of these stars could be a black hole. If so, the accretion disc will be particularly bright. The hole will actually steal matter away from its companion star.

This is probably all that you would see. Perhaps there would be some other matter in orbit around the hole. If you had the right instruments, you could know what the hole's electrical charge is, how fast it is rotating, and how much matter is inside it—but nothing else.

You could tell more about the black hole by going inside it. But if you went inside, you could never come back out.

You give orders to your first officer to steer the starship back into deep space. But somebody makes a miscalculation. The ship's computer announces that you are trapped inside the hole's gravitational field. Your engines are not powerful enough to pull away from it. You are being sucked into the hole. There is no way you can stop the ship from falling in.

Around the black hole is a sphere called the *event horizon*. This is the point beyond which light cannot escape, the point beyond which no events within the hole are visible. As your starship passed the event horizon, nothing would seem to have changed. You could still see the stars on the outside and still receive radio messages from the rest of the universe, though they would be distorted by the hole's intense gravity.

But you could not escape. And you would be invisible to anyone on the outside.

Scientists are not sure what happens in the middle of a black hole, but they suspect that it is very strange. When gravity becomes as strong as it does at the middle of a black hole, the laws of the universe begin to break down.

What does that mean? Nobody really knows. But Albert Einstein's famous General Theory of Relativity discusses the effects of intense gravitation.

One of Einstein's predictions was that time would slow down in a very strong gravitational field. On board your starship, your descent into the black hole would seem to take place quickly. But if someone could watch it happen from outside, it would seem to take place very slowly. As you neared the middle of the black hole, you would appear to an outsider to move more and more slowly, until you almost stopped altogether.

If you looked carefully enough at the rest of the universe, it would seem to be moving faster. Everything would be happening at an amazingly rapid pace.

What would happen as you reached the middle of the black hole? That's one of the great mysteries of the universe.

According to theory, there is no limit as to how far the collapse of an extremely large star can go. Theoretically it can keep on collapsing forever.

How can such a thing be possible? The star, like all matter in the universe, has size and mass. What happens to that mass as the star is crammed into a space infinitely small? Eventually, the matter at the middle of the hole will be smaller than the smallest particle in the smallest atom. It will be no larger than what mathematicians call a *point*, so small that it has no width or depth or height. Physicists refer to this extremely small piece of matter as a *singularity,* because there is no thing or place in the universe quite like it. And the natural laws that govern what takes place in the singularity are unique, unlike the natural laws in the rest of the universe.

No one knows what goes on in this singularity. Scientists admit that they cannot fully explain it. As you fall past the event horizon in your starship, you might become the first human being to find out what really happens at the heart of a black hole. But you wouldn't be able to report your discoveries to anyone on the *other* side of the event horizon.

Actually, you probably wouldn't find out. More likely, you would be torn apart by the gravitational tides, which are even stronger near a black hole than they are near a neutron star. By the time you reached the middle of the hole, the atoms of your starship would have been broken up into their smallest particles. You and your ship would become a part of the collapsing mass of the star. How far can you go before this happens? That depends on the size of the black hole itself. If it is very small, you would probably be torn apart by the tides before you even reached the event horizon. If it is a very large hole, you could go quite a distance before the tidal disaster took place. This is because the event horizon in a large hole is a very long distance from the strong gravitational forces in the middle. In either case, though, you would never reach the singularity.

But suppose you could somehow escape the gravitational tides. What would you find at the middle of a black hole?

Some scientists believe that you would find a gateway to other worlds.

It would seem that all the matter in the collapsing

star has to go *somewhere*. It has been theorized that it actually punches a hole in space and reappears somewhere else in the universe—or perhaps in another universe. As your starship nears the singularity, you may be able to enter that hole and cross vast distances in literally no time at all.

Where will you come out?

No one can say. You may find yourself farther away from Earth than our largest telescopes have ever seen. You would probably never be able to return.

The area in space where the matter from a black hole reappears might be called a *white hole*. All the matter from the collapsed star would explode outward from a single point, filling that section of space with brilliant light. The white hole would be a black hole running in reverse.

It would be a very spectacular sight. It should be visible from a great distance away. You might wonder if astronomers have ever seen objects in space that might be white holes.

They have. Such objects are called *quasars*.

CHAPTER THREE

Early in the twentieth century, an astronomer named Edwin Hubble made a startling discovery.

It had been known for years that stars tended to form together in *galaxies*. Galaxies are large groups of stars, often in the shape of spirals. Our own galaxy, which we call the Milky Way because of the way it looks in our skies, is one such spiral. So is the nearby Andromeda Galaxy. Some galaxies take the form of discs, some appear as spheres, others are irregular in shape. Two famous irregular galaxies are the Large and Small Magellanic Clouds, named after the famous Portuguese explorer Magellan, who observed them on his voyage around the tip of South America. They are clearly visible in the night sky of Earth's southern hemisphere, though not from the United States or the United Kingdom, which are in the northern hemisphere. They are the galaxies closest to our own.

The Milky Way Galaxy, its spiral shape clearly visible in this photograph.

A spiral galaxy in Andromeda*,*
seen edge on.

Just as stars gather together in galaxies, so galaxies themselves gather in *clusters*, or *groups*. Our own local group is made up of about twenty different galaxies, including the Andromeda Galaxy and the Magellanic Clouds. Some clusters are made up of thousands of galaxies.

In 1923 and 1924, Edwin Hubble was measuring the distances to nearby groups of galaxies and studying the light that they were producing. In studying this light, through an instrument called a *spectroscope,* he was able to analyze the elements from which the stars in these galaxies had formed. He discovered something odd. The light from these galaxies did not look the way it should. It had been changed by the *Doppler effect*.

What is the Doppler effect? It has to do with waves. You may know that sound is made up of waves, ripples that pass through the air the same way that ripples—waves—pass through water. When these waves reach our ears, our brains interpret them as sound. The kind of sound we hear depends on the distance between these waves. This distance is called the *wavelength*. If the distance between waves is long, we say that the sound has a long wavelength. If it is short, we say it has a short wavelength. The longer the wavelength, the deeper (or lower-pitched) the sound is. A sound with a very long wavelength would be interpreted by our brains as a low rumbling. The shorter the wavelength, the higher (or higher-pitched) the sound is. A sound with

A typical globular cluster of stars, this one located in the part of the universe known to astronomers as M3.

a very short wavelength would be interpreted by our brains as a shrill whistling.

The Doppler effect was discovered in 1842 by a scientist named Christian Doppler. Doppler found that if sound is produced by an object moving toward you, the sound waves become crowded together. If sound is produced by an object moving away from you, the sound waves become stretched out. This means that if a sound-producing object is moving toward you, the wavelength of the sound becomes shorter, because the distance between waves is less. If it is moving away from you, the wavelength of the sound becomes longer, because the distance between the waves is greater.

You've probably noticed that the siren of a fire engine seems shriller and higher-pitched as the engine moves toward you. By the opposite token, it becomes deeper as the engine moves away from you. This is because of the Doppler effect.

Visible light is not made up of waves, but the particles —called *photons*—of which it is made have many of the properties of waves. The wavelike particles are received by the eye, and the brain interprets them as different hues. The hue the brain "sees" depends on the wavelength of the light. If the wavelength is very short, the hue will be bluish; if long, it will be reddish. Like sound, light can be changed by the Doppler effect. When an object producing light (such as a star) is moving *toward* you, its wavelength becomes shorter; therefore we say it has become *blue-shifted*. When an object producing light is moving *away* from you, its wavelength becomes longer; therefore we say it has become *red-shifted*.

When Hubble looked at these distant galaxies, the ones beyond our local group, he discovered that they were *all* red-shifted. He assumed that this was caused by the Doppler effect. That meant that they were all moving away from us. Then he noticed that the farther away the galaxies were from us, the *more* red-shifted they were. If the red shift is a Doppler effect, that means that the farther away a galaxy is from us, the *faster* it is moving away.

This was true in every direction he looked. Every other galaxy is moving rapidly away from our own, except those in our local group. The farther those galaxies are from us, the faster they are moving.

Is Earth at the middle of some huge explosion? Is some invisible force pushing the rest of the universe away?

Not exactly. As far as we can tell, there *was* an explosion at some time in the distant past. Apparently, it sent everything in the universe expanding outward at great speeds. But Earth is not in the middle of it. Since every group of galaxies in the universe is speeding away from every *other* group of galaxies, it would look the same way no matter what galaxy you were watching this explosion from. At any point in the universe, it would seem as though all other groups of galaxies were hurtling away from you. It is impossible to pinpoint the middle of this *expanding universe*.

The explosion that caused this expansion probably took place between 10,000,000,000 and 20,000,000,000 years ago. Scientists refer to this explosion as the *Big Bang*. (This term was coined by the late physicist George Gamow.) It is believed that at one time all the matter in the universe was packed together into one huge mass. This is sometimes called the *primal egg*. (The word "primal" means "first" or "original.") This primal egg was so dense that it may not have been made up of atoms. It may not even have been made up of neutrons, as in a neutron star.

It may have been made up of *quarks,* the particles that some scientists believe are the basic building blocks of all matter. Quarks are even smaller than neutrons, protons, and electrons. For reasons that we do not fully understand, this primal egg exploded. The quarks joined together to form larger particles, which in turn joined together to form atoms. These atoms eventually grouped together to become galaxies, stars, planets, and everything else that now exists in the universe.

This explosion was so immense that astronomers can still detect its "echo" as radio waves in space. The effects of the explosion are still visible, as Hubble observed.

Most scientists believe that this expanding universe theory is true. If so, it explains Hubble's observations very neatly.

But in the 1960s astronomer A. R. Sandage made a discovery that didn't fit in with Hubble's red shift. Or, if it did, there was obviously a great deal about the universe we still didn't know.

Sandage found a number of dim stars that were the source of a large number of radio waves. These waves meant that the stars were producing a great deal of energy, much more than other astronomical objects of the same apparent size. When he examined these objects through a spectroscope, he discovered that they were extremely red-shifted.

According to Hubble's view of the universe, this red shift meant that these objects were rushing away from us. And because they were *very* red-shifted, they must be rushing away *very* quickly. According to the expanding universe theory, then, they must be very far away.

But astronomers realized quickly that if they were that far away, they must be more than just dim stars. To be seen over such a distance at all, they must be extremely bright.

Yet special instruments told scientists that these objects were not large—larger than stars, yes, but not as large as galaxies. How could they produce so much energy?

No one has yet been able to answer that question. No source of power known could make these so-called *quasi-stellar* ("starlike") *radio sources*—or *quasars,* for short—burn that brightly.

Could they be the other end of black hole tunnels through space? Could they be white holes?

Some experts believe this may be so. They believe that it is possible that the matter trapped inside black holes burrows its way out through a "wormhole" in space. These wormholes cut across to a distant part of the universe, where the compressed star matter bursts back out into space.

But it is only fair to point out that this is not the only possible explanation for the quasars. Astronomers have many theories as to their origins.

Some suspect that they are not as distant from us as is generally believed. If they are not as distant, then they are not as bright. You may have noticed that a bright light grows brighter as you get closer to it—and dimmer as you move away. A light bulb held a few inches (1 inch equals 2.5 cm) in front of your face is painful to look at, while the same light bulb a mile (1.6 km) away is barely visible. Therefore, the light we see coming from a star varies according to its distance. Since we have no direct means of measuring the actual brightness of a star (what astronomers call its *absolute magnitude*), we can only measure how bright it seems from Earth (its *apparent magnitude*).

If the quasars are not as far away as we think, there

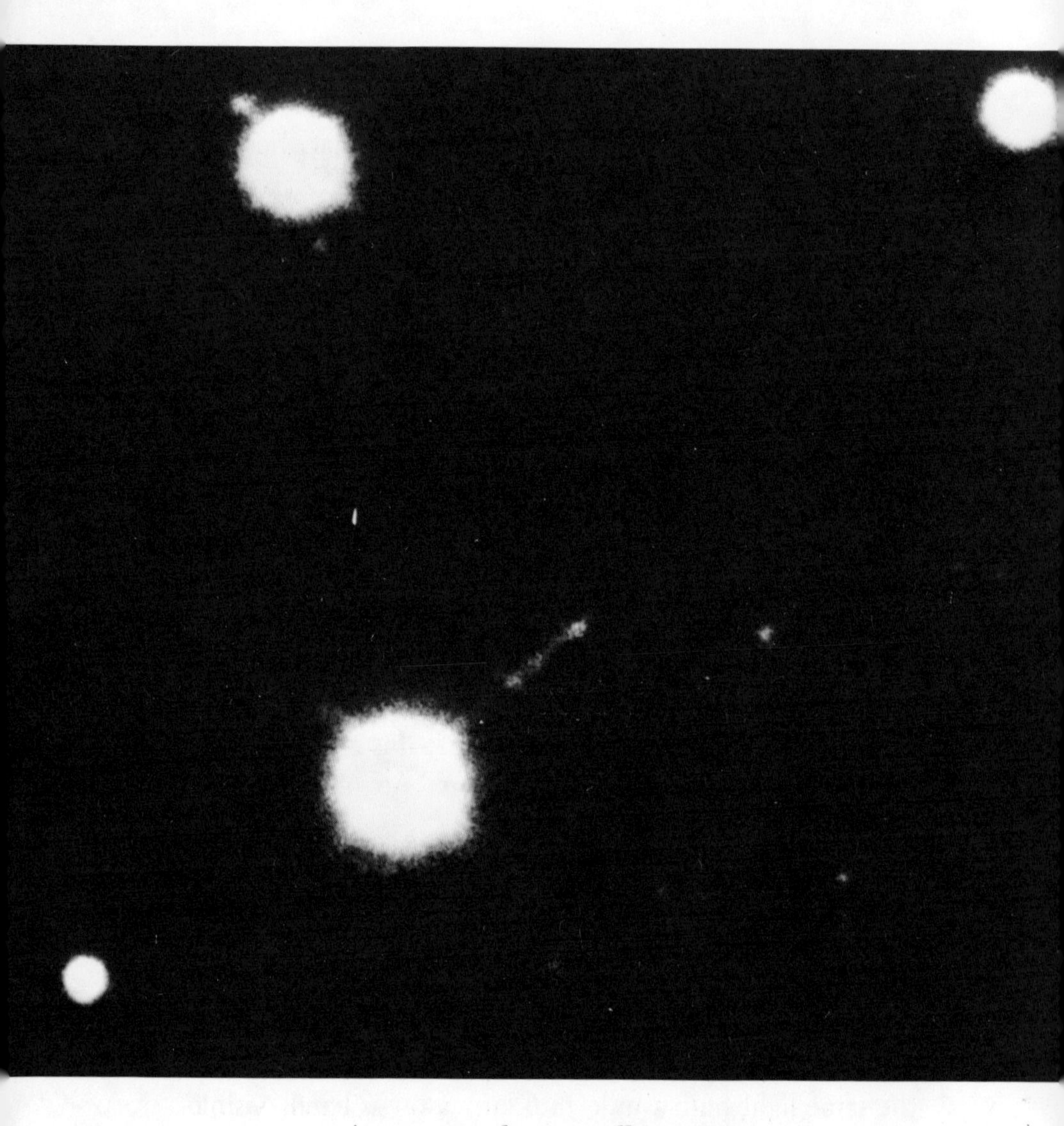

A quasar in the constellation Virgo. This object may produce a hundred thousand to a million times more infrared radiation than the total optical power of our entire Milky Way Galaxy. Several hundred such quasars are known to exist.

must be another reason for their extreme red shifts. Perhaps the quasars are not moving at the same speed as the rest of the expanding universe. Since Hubble, astronomers have assumed that all objects at the same distance from us in space are moving away from us at the same speed. Perhaps the quasars are moving away from Earth *faster* than other objects at the same distance.

It has been suggested that quasars might have been shot out of the midpoints of galaxies by great explosions, which have propelled them to very high speeds. There is some evidence for this theory. Galaxies have been observed with tremendous explosions taking place at their cores. These are called *Seyfert galaxies*, after the astronomer who discovered them. But if this is so, why are all the quasars *red*-shifted? The lack of blue-shifted quasars means that they are all rushing *away* from us. If they are really the results of galactic explosions, they should be moving in all directions. But they are not.

Perhaps the red shift is not caused by movement at all. According to Einstein's General Theory of Relativity, an intense gravitational field can produce a Doppler effect just as movement can. As the light struggles to escape the pull of gravity, its wavelength becomes longer and longer, as though it were being stretched by the intense gravitational attraction. In a sense this is what happens when a black hole forms. As the collapsing star becomes denser and denser and its gravity becomes greater and greater, the light becomes more and more red-shifted. Eventually it is red-shifted into invisibility. At that point the hole becomes truly black.

If the quasars are extremely dense objects, that could explain the red shifts. Their intense gravity would have the effect that Einstein described.

Another explanation is that quasars are galaxies in formation. When you look out into space, you are actually looking back in time. Because the light from the stars and galaxies takes a certain amount of time to reach Earth, we see them as they were when the light began its journey, not as they are now.

Light travels very rapidly—approximately 186,000 miles (299,000 km) every second. Space, however, is very vast. Even at this extremely rapid pace, the light from the star nearest to our solar system, Proxima Centauri, takes more than four years to reach us. The light from the nearest galaxy takes more than 150,000 years to get to Earth. The light from the Andromeda Galaxy takes over *2,000,000 years* to reach Earth—and Andromeda is still part of our local group of galaxies!

In fact, space is so vast that astronomers rarely measure it in miles. Instead, they measure it in *light-years*—the distance light travels in one year. A light-year is equal to roughly 6,000,000,000,000 miles (9,656,000,000,000 km). We would say, therefore, that Proxima Centauri is more than four light-years away. Andromeda is more than 2,000,000 light-years away. If the Hubble explanation of the quasar's distance is correct, quasars are billions of light-years from Earth. Because it takes the light from the quasars so long to reach us, we see them as they were billions of years ago. Since the universe is between 10,000,000,000 and 20,000,000,000 years old, we see the quasars as they were at a time closer to the Big Bang, nearer to the birth of the universe.

A *Seyfert galaxy.*

Quasars, then, may be galaxies in formation. No one knows if galaxy formation would produce the necessary amounts of power to explain quasars. Most scientists would say no, but the way in which galaxies are formed is not clearly understood. If nothing else, quasars indicate that the universe was very different when it was younger.

(It should be noted here that if quasars *are* the other ends of black hole tunnels, the tunnels may travel backwards in time as well as across space. Some theorists tell us that this may be possible.)

One of the most interesting theories draws a direct relationship between quasars and Seyfert galaxies. The theory suggests that both are galaxies in the process of collapsing rather than exploding, although that collapse also involves an explosion.

And that collapse is caused by black holes.

CHAPTER FOUR

Black holes can be dangerous—and not just to starships that fall into them.

A black hole floating alone in space will absorb anything that comes near. As it absorbs more and more matter, it grows larger and larger. Since space is never *completely* empty, black holes of more than a certain size are always absorbing matter. And growing.

How quickly a black hole grows depends on how much matter there is nearby. A black hole in a double star system may absorb a constant stream of matter from its companion star, until the companion has completely vanished.

In the previous chapter we saw that the nearest star is more than four light-years from Earth. The average distance between stars in this part of the galaxy is very great.

But in the middle of the galaxy, stars are much more tightly packed. In some places, there may be more than 100,000 stars within a single cubic light-year of space.

Some of these stars will eventually become black holes. Many of them may already have done so. If a normal star wanders too close to a star that has become a black hole, it will find itself torn apart by gravitational tides and sucked past the event horizon, trapped by the hole's gravitational field. Then it, too, will become part of the black hole.

And the hole will grow.

And as the hole grows, it will become more and more likely that other stars will be trapped by it. And as more stars are trapped, the hole will grow larger still.

Eventually there will be a giant black hole in the middle of the galaxy, a hole into which the entire galaxy may fall.

Many scientists believe that this is already happening in several galaxies that we can observe through telescopes. Some have even suggested that there is a giant black hole in the middle of *every* galaxy—including our own!

This is not as wild an idea as it sounds. If black holes exist, they are as likely to exist in the middle of a galaxy as anywhere else—in fact more likely, because there are more stars there. With so many black holes lurking within such a tightly packed mass of stars, collisions like the ones described above would be very likely to happen.

This may well explain the Seyfert explosions. As photographed through telescopes, the Seyferts are obviously the scene of violent activity. Some of them have jets of glowing matter shooting outward from their cores. At least one Seyfert is clearly associated with a chunk of matter that may have been ejected from it.

If the Seyferts are galaxies collapsing into black holes, that would explain a great deal.

As the stars in the middle of the galaxy are broken

apart by gravitational tides and drawn toward the event horizon, they would be heated to unbelievable temperatures. Tremendous amounts of energy would be released. Great amounts of radioactivity would be produced.

It would look a lot like a Seyfert galaxy.

Or a quasar.

It has been suggested that this may be the source of quasar energy as well. No one has been able to prove this. And it still doesn't explain why all the quasars are so far away.

If all galaxies are falling into giant black holes, our galaxy would be falling into a black hole too.

There is no direct evidence of this, but it is possible. We are unable to see the middle of our own galaxy because there are thick clouds of dust in the way. If it were exploding—or collapsing—we would not be able to see it happening.

However, even if our galaxy is collapsing into a black hole, there is no reason for us to worry about it. Our own sun is far out on the fringes of the galaxy. The collapse will not reach us for a long, long time, probably many billions of years. Our sun will have burned out long before then.

If large black holes can destroy galaxies, small ones can destroy planets.

Imagine a tiny black hole so small that it cannot be seen. If such a black hole collided with the planet Earth, it might easily pass right through Earth's surface and the mantle beneath. Black holes are so dense that solid ground would give way to them as easily as water.

If it were moving very fast, and its speed were great enough, the hole might simply pass right out through the other side of our planet. Otherwise, it would be trapped by Earth's gravitational field—or, looked at another way, Earth would be caught by the tiny hole's gravitational field.

If such a black hole were caught by Earth's gravity, it would begin absorbing matter from inside our world. And it would grow, slowly at first, then more and more quickly as it grew larger and larger.

Eventually our planet would collapse inward and disappear into the hole. Earth would no longer exist.

Is such a thing possible? Do such tiny black holes exist?

Black holes as small as the ones we are discussing could not form from the collapse of a star, because a star must have more than a certain amount of mass before it can become a black hole. But there could be some around that were formed in the time shortly after the Big Bang. The necessary pressures existed then.

In 1971, physicist Stephen Hawking suggested that the universe might be filled with tiny black holes. But more recently he has suggested that these holes no longer exist, that in the billions of years since the Big Bang they have evaporated.

Evaporated? How can a black hole evaporate?

According to Hawking and modern physics, it is possible for certain kinds of subatomic particles to escape from inside a black hole. Nothing larger can get out, but after billions of years of "leaking" particles, the tiny black holes would no longer exist.

Still, larger black holes (which absorb matter faster than they can leak) could create the sort of damage described above. But there are so few of them—relatively speaking—that it is unlikely that one will ever collide with Earth.

Or is it?

CHAPTER FIVE

Is it possible that Earth has already collided with a black hole?

We know that Earth still exists. It has not been swallowed by a hungry black hole. But could it not have collided with a hole moving fast enough to simply pass through one side of the planet and out the other?

Is there any indication that such a thing has ever happened?

Yes.

It was in this century, too. In Central Siberia.

On the morning of June 30, 1908, observers in China and Russia saw a great fireball (many claimed that it was actually shaped like a cylinder) pass across the sky. It struck ground in Russia, on the Central Siberian Plateau, near the Stony Tunguska River.

When it struck—or, more likely, just before it struck—it exploded. The explosion was as powerful as that of a

30-megaton hydrogen bomb, which means that the explosion had the force of 30,000,000 tons (27,000,000 m.t.) of TNT. A huge clap of sound was heard up to 500 miles (800 km) away. Observers reported a tall pillar of fire that rose far into the morning sky.

Buildings trembled hundreds of miles away. The Trans-Siberian Express, moving on a track a great distance from the core of the explosion, had to be brought to a halt, so great was the vibrating of the rails. An intense windstorm, marked by a savagely hot wind, blew across the hills. For weeks afterward, stunningly beautiful sunsets were seen all over the world.

Yet the explosion took place in such a remote part of the country that it was many years before the Russian authorities investigated.

Then, in 1927, an expedition of scientists made its way up the Stony Tunguska River through thick forests and swamps and intense cold. They found incredible devastation as they neared the site of the explosion. Many trees had been torn loose from the ground, their roots ripped from the earth. Other trees were stripped bare of their leaves. The ground all around was scorched, as if by intense heat.

And this was nineteen years after the explosion!

Near the middle of the devastated area, strange holes riddled the ground. The earth was misshapen and twisted; the ground looked, as one of the scientists put it, "like waves in water."

The expedition concluded that the explosion was caused by a meteorite.

In Arizona, near Winslow, there is a hole in the desert called Meteor Crater that is three-quarters of a mile (1.2 km) wide and 570 feet (175 m) deep. This hole was carved

Above: one site affected by the Siberian explosion. This area, located 30 miles (48 km) from where the explosion actually occurred, was once a dense forest. Right: Meteor Crater, near Winslow, Arizona.

out by a large meteorite that fell to Earth during prehistoric times. Such meteorites are cosmic debris, usually metallic, that are trapped by our planet's gravity and plunge into the Earth's atmosphere. The craters left behind by the impact of similar objects are plainly visible on the surface of the moon. Similar craters have been photographed on the planet Mars by space probes. Few such craters exist on Earth because meteorites usually burn up from friction in the atmosphere before they can reach the ground. And when they *do* reach Earth's surface, the craters they leave behind are quickly erased by wind and rain. (Since the moon has no atmosphere—and therefore no weather—there are many craters pitting its surface.)

The scientists who examined the scene of the Tunguska explosion in Siberia expected to find a crater, like the one in Arizona or the ones on the moon. They did not. There was no crater, only the small holes pocking the ground and the destruction left by the explosion. Most meteorites leave behind metallic remains. Explorers could find none in Siberia.

There are many theories as to the cause of the Tunguska explosion. Many scientists accept the meteorite explanation, but without a crater or some kind of physical evidence, this theory remains unsubstantiated. And no one can fully explain why, if it was a meteorite, it exploded as it did.

A second theory is that Earth collided with a comet. Comets are chunks of ice and dust that orbit the sun. Their orbits are oddly shaped, so that they can come very close to the sun at one point in their orbit, then shoot back out into the depths of space. As they approach the sun, they emit a long, glowing tail of excited particles. Because comets are mostly ice, a comet striking the Tunguska region would have left behind no physical remains. But observers who saw the falling Tunguska object said that it did not resemble a comet.

Another theory supposes that it was a meteorite, but a meteorite made of *antimatter*. Antimatter is a substance that scientists have long theorized and even created in laboratories but have never discovered in nature. Antimatter is in every way the opposite of normal matter, so much so that the two cannot exist together in the same place. If antimatter comes into contact with matter, the two destroy one another in a huge explosion. That would explain what had happened over the Siberian forests: The antimatter would have exploded on contact with Earth's thick lower atmosphere, which is made of normal matter. (The upper atmosphere, also made of normal matter, would have been too thin to cause the meteorite to explode.) It would also explain the lack of physical remains.

One of the most interesting explanations is that the Tunguska object was a spaceship. Theorists point to the fact that the disastrous explosion took place in a remote location, with absolutely no loss of life and almost no loss of property. If the Tunguska object was a simple meteorite, it could have struck anywhere on Earth. If it had struck in the ocean, it would have caused tidal waves and disastrous flooding all over the world. If it had struck the ice caps, it would have caused melting, which in turn would have caused flooding. If it had struck in a populated area, millions of people would have died. But it struck in one of the few places on Earth where it could do no damage at all. Could someone have deliberately steered it to remote Siberia? Noting the resemblance of the Tunguska explosion to that of a hydrogen bomb, theorists have suggested that the spaceship might have been a nuclear-powered one.

The devastation, therefore, would have been created by the explosion of its engines.

Finally, it has been offered that the Tunguska object was a black hole. The intense gravitational field of a very small black hole would have been enough to twist the ground into the patterns observed by the 1927 expedition and to cause the destruction around the site. It would then have passed through Earth and come out somewhere in the middle of the ocean, on the far side of the planet. It would have created a huge geyser of water as it came back out, but in the middle of the ocean this would not have been seen.

However, the geyser would probably have caused tidal waves and flooding in coastal regions. Nothing like this was reported. And there should have been measurable radiation left at the site of the explosion.

None of these theories can be proven, given our current state of knowledge. Most of them fail to explain *all* of the observed facts. Yet all of them provide food for thought.

We may never know the true cause of the Tunguska explosion. One thing is certain, however. If it *was* caused by a black hole, it must have passed all the way through Earth. If it had not, there would be no Earth left!

CHAPTER SIX

How did we find out about black holes?

Most of what we know about black holes—and neutron stars—has been worked out theoretically by scientists. Their theories are based on what we have learned about the universe from observation.

The first person to conceive of the idea behind black holes was the French mathematician and astronomer Pierre Simon de Laplace. Laplace knew nothing of the principle of gravitational collapse, but in 1798 he predicted that a star with a great enough mass could vanish from sight. Its gravity would be so intense that light would be unable to escape from its surface. Laplace imagined these black holes as being extremely large, rather than the extremely compressed objects we now believe them to be. Such a star would have to have a diameter of about 200,000,000 miles (320 million km)—roughly the same diameter as Earth's orbit around the sun—but unlike actual giant stars it would be about as dense as our sun. Those giant stars that really *do* exist are thin and gaseous and therefore do not have strong enough gravitational fields to become black holes. A star as large and dense as Laplace imagined could not exist in the real world. Instead, it would collapse under its own weight and become a *real* black hole. But Laplace, as we noted above, did not know about gravitational collapse.

No one did, until the discovery of Sirius B.

Sirius is one of the stars closest to Earth, only eight light-years away, and it has the greatest apparent magnitude of any star in the sky. (This means, as you'll recall, that we *see* it as being brighter than any other star. This *apparent* brightness is partially due to its closeness to Earth, though it *is* a large star.) In 1844, Friedrich Wilhelm Bessel discovered that Sirius' position in space wobbled slightly. This wobbling motion was not visible to the naked eye but could be detected through long study by telescope. It was as though Sirius were being affected by a powerful gravitational field. Yet no source of such a field could be seen.

Bessel decided that there was a very large, dark planet in orbit around Sirius—or perhaps a star that for some reason emitted no light. This unseen planet or star became known as the "dark companion" of Sirius.

In 1862, however, Alvin Clark discovered a very dim star in orbit around Sirius. The dark companion was not dark after all.

This was very puzzling to scientists. They knew that the companion star must be very massive because of its

Three exposures of Sirius A, showing the companion star, Sirius B.

gravitational effect on Sirius. Why, then, did Sirius B (as the companion was now called) shine so dimly? Scientists measured the temperature of the dim star by using a spectroscope and found that it was extremely hot, which meant that it must be shining very brightly, almost as brightly as Sirius. Yet Sirius, which was the same distance from Earth, shone many, many times brighter. The only way Sirius B could be both hot and dim was if it were very small.

This left astronomers more confused than ever. Judging by the gravitational effect Sirius B had on Sirius A, they knew it was very massive, and therefore they assumed it was very large. Judging by the amount of light it was producing, they knew it was very small. How could it be both large and small at the same time?

The only possible explanation was that Sirius B contained the same mass as a large star, but that the mass was crammed into a very small space. Sirius B had to be extremely dense. It had to be denser than any matter previously known, so dense that a spoonful would weigh several tons.

Scientists had made all of these calculations by the end of the nineteenth century, but the results were difficult to accept. Sirius B was a new kind of star. Astronomers called it a white dwarf. In Chapter One we saw how such stars come into existence.

In 1916, physicist Karl Schwarzschild picked up the concept developed by Laplace more than a century earlier, that a strong enough gravitational field could trap even light in its intense pull. Working with equations from Einstein's General Theory of Relativity, Schwarzschild calculated the distance from an intense gravitational field beyond which light could not escape. This distance is called the *Schwarzschild radius*.

Much of the early work on the subject of gravitational collapse was performed by an astronomer named Subrahmanyan Chandrasekhar. Chandrasekhar—or Chandra, as he is better known in the astronomical world—discovered that stars with more than a certain amount of mass cannot exist as white dwarfs. The mass beyond which the dwarfs could not exist, known as *Chandrasekhar's limit*, was 1.4 times the mass of our sun. If there is more mass than this, the star will continue collapsing beyond the white dwarf stage, possibly becoming what we now know to be a neutron star.

This does not mean that stars more than 1.4 times the size of our sun cannot become white dwarfs. Most stars lose a great deal of their mass before collapsing—during the supernova explosion, for instance.

J. Robert Oppenheimer, working with Chandra's equations, realized that an even larger star (one with more than 3.2 times the mass of our sun at the time of collapse) could *never* stop collapsing. It would become what we now know as a black hole.

In 1939, scientists were not yet ready to accept this concept. One particularly distinguished astronomer called this theory a *reductio ad absurdum* (an argument carried to the point of absurdity).

It has only been since the early 1960s—with the work of such theorists as Kip Thorne of the California Institute of Technology and Stephen Hawking, the young British theorist mentioned earlier—that black hole theory has been generally accepted by the scientific community.

It is Hawking who has done much of the work at the very fringes of black hole theory. Some observers of the scientific scene believe Hawking to be as great a force in theoretical physics as Einstein. Hawking, nearly paralyzed

and confined to a wheelchair by a disease of the nervous system, nevertheless developed the theory of mini-black holes that might have been formed at the time of the Big Bang and calculated that such black holes would by now have "leaked" away into space, as we discussed in Chapter Four.

CHAPTER SEVEN

All right, so black holes look good on paper. But have we actually seen one?

By definition, of course, a black hole *cannot* be seen; that is, it cannot be detected by our eyes (and therefore by our optical telescopes) because it emits no light. There are certain things about a black hole that can be learned in *other* ways, however. To understand how this can be, we must first discuss the revolution that has taken place in the field of astronomy over the last few decades.

The first astronomers did not have telescopes. They looked toward the sky with their naked eyes and studied the movements of the stars and planets.

At first they could not even write down what they had observed, because writing had not yet been invented. They passed all astronomical knowledge down by word of

mouth from generation to generation. Later, they recorded it on tablets and scrolls and, *much* later, in books.

Those early astronomers observed the way stars moved across the sky and divided those stars into *constellations*. They noted that certain stars moved at a different pace from the others, and they called these *planets*, from a Greek word meaning "wanderers." (Later, it was discovered that these were not stars at all but worlds in orbit around the sun. In fact, our own Earth is one such planet.)

All of these observations came to these astronomers by a single channel: visible light. The light from these stars and planets would travel through space. Some of it reached Earth, where it could be seen by anyone who looked up at the sky on a clear night.

When the telescope was invented, it proved to be a great boon to astronomers. A telescope magnifies astronomical objects and draws in more light than the naked eye. New planets and stars were discovered, as well as galaxies and great clouds of dust and gas. A great revolution occurred in the field of astronomy. Suddenly a great deal more about the universe was understood than had ever been understood before.

Yet visible light is not the only way in which we can receive information about the stars. There are radio waves, for instance, and X rays. Both of these, like light, are forms of radiation. They can be received through special instruments. And they can tell us a great deal about the universe.

An early telescope that caused a sensation in England in 1790.

Radio waves from space were discovered in 1931 by Karl Guthe Jansky of the Bell Telephone Laboratories. The first antenna designed to receive this radiation was built in 1936.

After World War II, many such *radio telescopes* were built. These were designed to detect radiation given off by a number of astronomical objects and to tell us things about those objects that earlier forms of astronomy could not.

The development of radio telescopes is considered the beginning of the second great revolution in the field of astronomy.

In 1967, a young graduate student named Jocelyn Bell detected bursts of radio waves on the new radio telescope at Cambridge University Observatory. The bursts lasted one-twentieth of a second each and were received every 1.33730109 seconds.

The bursts came at such regular intervals that some people suspected they were signals from intelligent beings. These beings were termed *LGM's*, for "Little Green Men," though this possibility was never really taken seriously.

Anthony Hewish, director of the observatory, theorized that the bursts were coming from some kind of *pulsating star*. This term was quickly shortened to *pulsar*.

A radio telescope. Radio telescopes ushered in the second revolution in the world of astronomy.

Charts of earlier observations were searched and three more pulsars were located. Over a hundred more have been discovered since.

What *are* pulsars? What astronomical body could produce such regular bursts of radiation?

An astronomer named Thomas Gold suggested that they might be neutron stars. Neutron stars had been theorized by J. Robert Oppenheimer years before, but there had been no evidence that they actually existed.

If neutron stars rotated, as theorists were almost certain they did, they would rotate very quickly. (Smaller objects tend to rotate more quickly than larger ones, because it requires less energy to make them rotate. The small neutron star would at one time have been a normal-size star and it would still have the rotational energy of the large star. This means it would rotate much faster than it did before its collapse.) If they rotated fast enough, they might actually *fling* energy off into space. This would account for the radio waves that Bell had detected.

But how could this theory be proven?

Neutron stars are the corpses of stars that have exploded and collapsed. If we could identify a location in space where we know that a star had once exploded, we could search for a pulsar there. If we found one, it would be strong evidence that pulsars and neutron stars are the same thing.

The Crab Nebula has long been believed to be the shell of a star that exploded in the year A.D. 1054. We know the date because the explosion was observed by Chinese astronomers at the time. The Crab Nebula is an expanding cloud of gas and dust, apparently flung off by the dying star.

And when astronomers turned their radio telescopes on the Crab Nebula, they found a pulsar there.

In 1969, astronomers identified a dim star where the pulsar should be. Its light flashes on and off with the same rhythm as the radio pulses. Astronomers believe that they are observing the weak light produced by the neutron star.

What about black holes? Is there a way to detect black holes?

We saw earlier how black holes are often surrounded by a spiral of glowing matter heated by gravitational energy and known as an accretion disc. Some of this matter falls into the hole. Some of it remains in orbit. If the black hole is in the vicinity of another star, the accretion disc will be extremely thick and bright.

This matter is heated to such high temperatures that it emits a form of radiation known as X *rays*. If these X rays are strong enough, they will travel across space to Earth. Only a black hole in a double star system would have a thick enough accretion disc to produce X rays this intense.

X rays cannot pass through our planet's atmosphere, but they can be detected by sensitive instruments on board satellites orbiting beyond the atmosphere.

In the mid-1960s, a very strong source of X rays was discovered in the constellation Cygnus. That source is known as Cygnus X-1. At first the radiation was believed to come from a neutron star, but changes in the intensity of the X rays made this unlikely. Visual astronomers working with radio astronomers located the source of the radiation near a visible star.

Astronomers studied the motion of the visible star, known as HD-226868, and decided that the star was part

The Crab Nebula, in the constellation Taurus.

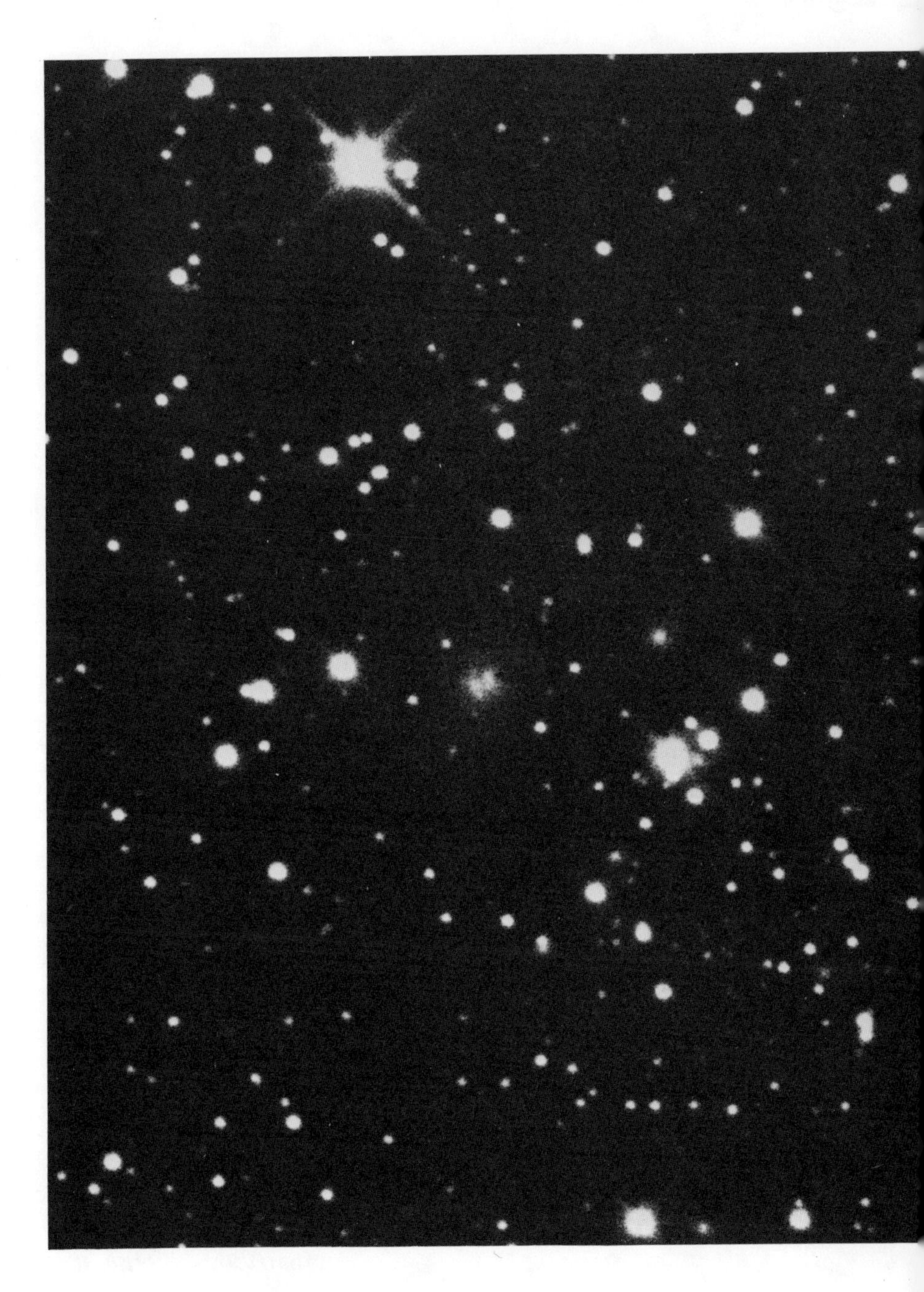

The galaxy where Cygnus X-1 is located.

of a double star system. However, its companion star was not visible. Apparently the invisible companion star was the source of the X rays.

In order for the radiation from Cygnus X-1 to reach Earth, it must be producing more than 1,000,000,000 times as much energy as our own sun. Many astronomers believe that only a black hole, with its intense gravitational field, could produce that sort of energy.

The evidence points in that direction. Astronomers can guess at the size of the invisible companion of HD-226868 by studying the effect it has on the visible star. Their conclusion is that it must be a very massive star. In fact, observations tell us that it is almost nine times as massive as our sun. And yet it cannot be seen!

More recently, astronomers have discovered what they believe to be a black hole swallowing a galaxy!

The galaxy is known as M-87. For some time, observers had noticed that it was emitting a dim streak of light from its core. Now it is believed that the galaxy contains a small, dark object 10,000,000,000 times as massive as our sun!

Very sensitive instruments indicate that the stars that make up the core of M-87 are moving very rapidly. The only likely explanation for this movement is the presence of a very powerful gravitational field. However, there are

M87. This exposure shows a nuclear jet trailing out from the main body of the star.

An artist's concept of NASA's space telescope, to be launched into orbit in the 1980s.

not enough stars visible in M-87 to account for this gravitation. Whatever is creating this force must be dark and therefore invisible.

Although it has not yet been proven, the most likely explanation for the missing mass in M-87 is that a black hole lurks at the heart of the galaxy. The amount of radio waves and X rays emitted by the galaxy indicates that this may well be the case.

Some theorists even believe that M-87 was at one time a quasar—or may become one in the future!

How can a very massive star escape detection? Only, some scientists feel, if it is a black hole.

Several more *X-ray binaries* (as double star systems are known) have been discovered since Cygnus X-1. One of the most recent of these, at this writing, is V861 Sco, an X-ray source in the constellation of Scorpius.

It is known that V861 is a double star system, with one visible star and an unseen companion. It is believed that the companion is massive enough to be a black hole. Though the X rays from V861 are not terribly intense, they have been observed to disappear completely at regular intervals, probably as the dark companion passes behind the visible star.

Since the X-ray source, judging from its effect on the visible star, has twelve to fourteen times the mass of our sun, it is unlikely that it could be anything but a black hole.

Until a more advanced method of visual astronomy is developed, it might not be possible to prove that these objects are what they seem to be—black holes. However, in the early to mid-1980s, NASA plans to launch a space telescope into orbit around Earth. Without our planet's atmosphere to interfere with our view of the sky, this telescope should open untold wonders to astronomers' eyes. Perhaps then the question of whether black holes actually exist will be answered once and for all.

CHAPTER EIGHT

Let us assume that black holes *do* exist. The evidence seems to indicate that this is so, even if there is no absolute proof.

If black holes exist, what good will this knowledge do us?

As long as we remain in the immediate vicinity of the planet Earth, we are unlikely to have any direct encounters with black holes. (Unless, of course, one encounters us, as may have happened in the Tunguska incident.) However, when humanity does at last venture out into deep space—the space between the star systems and galaxies—the possibility of literally running into a black hole will be very real.

Obviously black holes will be hazards for space explorers. A starship in the vicinity of a black hole will run the risk of being destroyed by gravitational tides, not to mention the risk of being trapped behind the event horizon, as we saw in Chapter Two.

And yet could there be ways in which black holes could prove useful to us?

Yes. Several of them. Theorists have come up with a number of possible uses for black holes. Some of these uses may sound comical, others difficult to understand. But you must realize that *all* of these are only possibilities. We won't know what can *really* be done with a black hole until we *find* one.

One suggestion that might turn out to be more useful than it sounds is to use black holes as interstellar garbage dumps.

The usefulness of this should be at least partially obvious. Instead of polluting our own planet or other planets or even outer space, we could hurl our waste past the event horizon of a black hole. We would never see it again. A black hole would be the most efficient disposal unit ever known. The trash would be compacted into the smallest size possible and could not possibly return from the hole.

Surprisingly, this would allow us to turn our garbage into energy. The heat produced by gravitational collapse in the accretion disc is one of the most effective methods of energy production in the universe. It would produce far more energy than any other method available. Black holes, then, could serve as the answer to some future energy crisis.

Or perhaps small black holes could serve as a means of sending messages via gravity waves across great distances in space. If we could harness a black hole properly, we could turn it into a gravity wave generator.

How would we go about harnessing a black hole? Well, we know that all black holes have an electrical charge. Perhaps that means that they can be controlled by magnets. Or perhaps we can somehow grip them by using their own intense gravitational force. By "wiggling" a captive black hole, we could produce our own gravity waves, thus producing a signal that could be detected across great distances.

Perhaps the most dramatic use of black holes would be as highways in the sky, tunnels across the universe. We discussed earlier the possibility that the matter trapped inside a black hole could form a "wormhole" in space. Such a passageway would be created by the enormous compression of matter at the middle of the hole. Unable to stop growing denser, but with nowhere else to go, the matter bursts free of the hole and reappears somewhere else in the universe, in a white hole.

According to Einstein's Special Theory of Relativity, it is impossible for ordinary matter to move at speeds greater than or equal to that of light. (Some theorists believe that there are particles called *tachyons* that can *only* move faster than the speed of light.) You will recall that the speed of light is about 186,000 miles (299,000 km) a second. Even if we could build spaceships that moved at speeds close to that of light, it would take more than four years to travel to the nearest star and more than 2,000,000 years to reach the Andromeda Galaxy. And it is unlikely that spaceships capable of moving even *that* fast will be developed in the next century or so.

Therefore, using ordinary means of space travel (if space travel can be called ordinary), the human race is never likely to travel farther than the very nearest stars, if that far. The journey to more-distant stars would take too long. Even a radio message sent from the nearest star would take years to arrive on Earth.

However, travel through a black hole would be instantaneous. It would take no time at all. No sooner would you enter one end of the wormhole than you would arrive at the other. The trip would not take place in ordinary space, so it would not be subject to Einstein's restrictions. At least this is what many physicists believe.

By entering a black hole and jumping to the nearest white hole, we could cross space in a series of great leaps. We could go anyplace where there were white and black holes.

The British science writer Adrian Berry has written a book entitled *The Iron Sun,* in which he proposes that a network of white and black holes be *constructed* across the universe. Berry displays this scheme in some detail.

His construction plan involves the heating of clouds of hydrogen with laser beams. When the hydrogen becomes extremely hot its atomic structure changes and it can be influenced by magnets. Spaceships generating powerful magnetic fields could fly through rich interstellar gas clouds, much like the ones from which stars form, and harvest the hydrogen they contain. The ships would pile this hydrogen into a huge mass, until it collapsed under its own gravitational weight. More and more matter could be piled onto this mass until it reached black hole density and disappeared behind its event horizon. Berry calculates that a black hole could be built in about fifteen years.

To enable the system to operate on a two-way basis, Berry suggests that mechanical construction equipment, controlled by computer, be sent through this black hole so that it can build *another* black hole at the other end of the wormhole. This second hole would allow future astronauts to return to the vicinity of Earth.

Certainly a network like this could be the basis of a galactic, or even universal, civilization. In his book *The Cosmic Connection,* astronomer Carl Sagan suggests that galactic civilizations in space may already exist, congregated around black holes, just as early civilizations on Earth developed around rivers. And when humanity discovers its first black hole, it may well become part of this galactic civilization as well.

CHAPTER NINE

Is it possible that we are living inside a black hole?

We know, of course, that our sun is not a collapsing star. And Earth is hardly dense enough to keep us from escaping into space. Yet some scientists believe that the universe itself, including all of the galaxies and stars that we see in our telescopes and even those we cannot see, may be a black hole—a black hole from which nothing can escape, a black hole that may eventually collapse.

In Chapter Three we discussed the Big Bang theory. According to this theory, the universe began as an extremely dense lump of matter that exploded. The result of this explosion is the universe we see today, still expanding outward from its midpoint.

What if that primal lump of matter was a black hole? What if it had been so dense that even light could not escape from it, not without eventually falling back in?

That would mean that even though the universe is expanding now, that expansion must eventually come to an end. The stars and galaxies flung outward in that original explosion will eventually have to fall back to the middle of the universe, because they will never be able to escape completely from that hole. In the end, the universe will once again form one huge, extremely dense lump of matter.

This is called the *oscillating universe theory*. It assumes that the universe has been exploding, collapsing, and reforming forever and will keep on doing so forever.

Scientists find this theory attractive because it eliminates some questions that they cannot answer: Where did that original lump of matter come from? Why was all that matter packed together into the primal egg, waiting to explode? According to the oscillating universe theory, it was there as the result of the collapse of another universe, which had formed as the result of the explosion of a lump of matter left over from the collapse of yet another universe, and so on, for all of eternity. This saves scientists from having to explain where the matter originally came from, because the oscillating universe theory suggests that it has been there forever, exploding and collapsing, exploding and collapsing, with no real beginning.

Unfortunately, there is no proof that this is so. It sounds nice, like something that really should have happened, but the evidence actually points in the opposite direction.

Astronomers have a pretty good idea of the rate at which the universe is expanding, though the precise figure is always being refined. They can make an educated guess as to how long the universe has been expanding. And, by studying the stars and galaxies, they can make a rough guess at how much mass there is in the universe.

If their calculations about that last figure are correct, there just isn't enough matter in the universe to make it a black hole.

You might wonder how the universe could be a black hole at all. It's not very dense, certainly not as dense as the black holes discussed in earlier chapters. But you might remember that the larger a black hole is, the less dense it has to be.

Laplace's black hole, for instance, had the density of an ordinary star, yet its great size gave it the properties of a black hole. For an object the size of the universe, very little density would be required to create a black hole.

But astronomers still aren't sure that the density of the universe is even *that* great. To be a true black hole, it would need more mass than astronomers can find. The amount of extra mass required to make our universe a black hole is often referred to as the *missing mass.*

If this missing mass exists, where could it be? Ironically, some theorists think it may be hiding in black holes. Since black holes cannot be seen through telescopes, it is difficult for astronomers to take them into account when estimating the amount of matter in the universe. However, generally accepted estimates of the number of black holes in the universe *still* would not account for the missing mass.

Some scientists believe that there is a giant black hole in the middle of every galaxy. This makes a great deal of sense, as we saw in Chapter Four. If true, it might explain where the missing mass is hiding.

If the oscillating universe theory is ever proved, scientists will be very happy. The idea of a universe constantly forming and reforming is a very attractive one.

In Chapter Two we discussed the idea of a singularity and saw how the laws of science break down in the middle of a black hole. No one knows what form this breakdown takes. Probably, no one *can* know without actually going to the middle of a black hole and observing what happens there. As far as we know at this time, all singularities are hidden behind event horizons, where they cannot be seen. And no one who passes beyond an event horizon can return.

Yet physicist Stephen Hawking has shown that it is possible for matter to "leak" out of a black hole. The matter is in the form of elementary particles, but those particles can form larger particles once they enter normal space. And according to Hawking these particles can take almost any form.

It is interesting to consider what this means. If the matter ejected from a black hole can take any form, it is possible that *anything* can come out of a black hole. Anything. Strange objects, hideous creatures, spaceships, palm trees, or grandfather clocks. You or I could come out of a black hole. Gold and jewels could come out of a black hole. Anything at all. Anything.

Of course, it is very unlikely that anything like that will come out. But there are a lot of black holes. And they will be around for a long, long time. . . .

It's even more interesting to consider that if the universe is a giant black hole, it once had a singularity in its middle. Maybe it still does.

Scientists have a great deal of difficulty studying the origin of the universe. They have a pretty good idea of how matter formed out of all the particles contained in the primal egg. But they don't know *why* the egg was there. Or why it exploded.

Maybe scientists have trouble explaining the origin of

our universe because they are trying to explain it with the *laws* of our universe. Maybe things were different then, in that first fraction of a second that our universe existed. In the beginning our universe may have been a singularity. And the laws of nature are different in a singularity. Strange things can happen.

And, when you think about it, what could be stranger than the universe that was formed in that primal explosion?

We take our world for granted. We were born here, after all. We grew up with trees and air and water and skies that grow dark at night and light during the day and creatures that walk and crawl on the land and swim in the sea and fly through the air. And we grew up with the most incredible things of all: human beings, with the intelligence and sense to study that world and wonder about it and even to take it for granted.

And if you know much about the universe, you probably take it for granted that there are stars and planets and galaxies. And even black holes.

Yet why should these things be? Why should the universe be the way it is? Why should there be stars and galaxies and plants and trees? Why should there be life and intelligence and day and night and gravity and energy? Isn't that the most incredible thing?—that the universe should be the way it is? That it should *be* at all?

Maybe we owe that to the primal singularity, the one that may have existed at the heart of the Big Bang. Maybe, in that one incredibly small, incredibly compressed packet of matter, where anything at all could happen, the strangest thing of all took place.

Our universe was born.

SUGGESTED READINGS

Asimov, Isaac. *The Collapsing Universe: The Story of Black Holes*. New York: Walker & Company, 1977.

———. *How Did We Find Out About Black Holes?* New York: Walker & Company, 1978.

———. *To the Ends of the Universe*. rev. ed. New York: Walker & Company, 1976.

Berger, Melvin. *Planets, Stars, and Galaxies*. New York: G. P. Putnam's Sons, 1978.

Berry, Adrian. *The Iron Sun: Crossing the Universe Through Black Holes*. New York: E. P. Dutton & Co., 1977.

Branley, Franklin Mansfield. *The Milky Way: Galaxy Number One*. New York: Thomas Y. Crowell Co., 1969.

Freeman, Mae and Ira. *The Sun, the Moon, and the Stars*. rev. ed. New York: Random House, 1979.

Mitton, Jacqueline and Simon. *Concise Book of Astronomy*. Englewood Cliffs, N. J.: Prentice-Hall, 1978.
Zim, Herbert Spencer. *The Universe*. newly rev. ed. New York: William Morrow & Co., 1973.

You might also be interested in the following science fiction titles:

Niven, Larry. *Hole in Space*. New York: Ballantine Books, 1976.
———. *Neutron Star*. New York: Ballantine Books, 1975.
———. *Tales of Known Space: The Universe of Larry Niven*. New York: Ballantine Books, 1975.
———. *A World Out of Time*. New York: Holt, Rinehart & Winston, 1976.
Pohl, Frederik. *Gateway*. New York: St. Martins' Press, 1977.
Pournelle, Jerry, ed. *Black Holes*. New York: Fawcett, 1979.

INDEX

Page numbers in italics indicate illustrations.

ABOUT THE AUTHOR

Christopher Lampton is a free-lance writer specializing in science and science fiction, though his early training was in communications and theatre.

Chris is the author of four science fiction novels, the most recent of which is Gateway to Limbo *(Doubleday).*

He lives in Hyattsville, Maryland.